Jeden Tag ein bisschen besser

W0321220

ENGLISCH

Vokabeltrainer

6. Schuljahr

von
Ingrid Preedy
Brigitte Seidl

Illustriert von
Roland Beier

Cornelsen
SCRIPTOR

Die Autorinnen:
Ingrid Preedy ist Britin. Sie hat langjährige Erfahrung als Englischlehrerin und ist in der Lehrerfortbildung tätig.
Sie ist Autorin mehrerer Schulbücher und Unterrichtsmaterialien.
Brigitte Seidl verfügt über 20-jährige Berufserfahrung als Englisch-, Deutsch- und Sportlehrerin. Auch sie ist Autorin mehrerer Lehrwerke und Unterrichtsmaterialien.

Cornelsen online http://www.cornelsen.de

Bibliografische Information: Die Deutsche Bibliothek verzeichnet diese Publikation in der Deutschen Nationalbibliografie; detaillierte bibliografische Daten sind im Internet über http://dnb.ddb.de abrufbar.

Dieses Werk berücksichtigt die Regeln der reformierten Rechtschreibung und Zeichensetzung.

5. 4. 3. 2. 1. Die letzten Ziffern bezeichnen
09 08 07 06 05 Zahl und Jahr der Auflage.

Redaktion: Annegret Hauser, Berlin
Satz/Layout/Herstellung: Beate Schubert, Berlin
Illustrationen: Roland Beier, Berlin
Umschlagentwurf: Bauer + Möhring, Berlin,
unter Verwendung einer Illustration von Roland Beier
Druck und Bindearbeiten: Saaledruck Naumburg
Printed in Germany
ISBN 3-589-22071-6
Bestellnummer 220716

Gedruckt auf säurefreiem Papier, umweltschonend hergestellt aus chlorfrei gebleichten Faserstoffen.

Inhalt

Vorwort

Hallo, liebe Schülerinnen und Schüler!
Hallo, liebe Eltern!

Wer **jeden Tag ein bisschen besser** wird, ist bald sehr gut!

Dieses Heft stellt auf jeder Doppelseite ein Thema aus dem Englischunterricht der 6. Klasse vor, das in einer Viertel- bis halben Stunde bearbeitet werden kann. Eine Doppelseite pro Tag genügt völlig.
Man schreibt einfach direkt ins Heft rein. Ist einmal nicht genug Platz, kann auch alles auf ein Blatt Papier geschrieben werden.

In der Mitte des Heftes haben wir einen Lösungsteil zum Heraustrennen eingeheftet. Damit sollen immer gleich die Ergebnisse überprüft werden! Das ist ganz wichtig, um in Zukunft Fehler zu vermeiden!

Viel Spaß und viel Erfolg!

1 Holidays

Das Datum von heute ____________

Planning a trip; a secret code

Alex träumt von einer Weltreise in den großen Ferien.
Schreibe auf, was er träumt.

A trip around the world would be fantastic!

1. I'd like to ______________________ in Whistler in Canada.
2. I'd like to ______________________ in the Yosemite Park in the USA.
3. I'd like to ______________________ in Denmark.
4. I'd like to ______________________ in Italy.
5. I'd like to ______________________ of the Great Wall in China.
6. I'd like to ______________________ in Africa.
7. I'd like to ______________________ in Australia.
8. I'd like to ______________________ in New Zealand.

Um sich seinen Traum zu erfüllen, schaut er einen Urlaubskatalog durch. Setze die fehlenden Wörter ein.
hotels – holiday apartment – campsite – farm – youth hostel – house boat

Book with us!
We have got great accomodation* for everybody.

a) You love nature and you have got your own tent, then stay at the „Woodland ________________." **b)** A ______________________ is the right place for young people who haven't got a lot of money and who like to meet people from all over the world. **c)** You can book a ________________________ when you need a kitchen and two bedrooms for your whole family. Then you can have dinner whenever you want. **d)** Your children love to feed or to play with animals? Then spend a holiday on a __________. **e)** You like to be as close to the water as possible. Then why not spent some days and nights on a very nice ____________________ ? **f)** A great way to relax is to stay for a week in one of our many ___________ where you can have a room with a private bath. Breakfast and dinner are included in the price.

**accomodation* = Unterkunft

Alex schreibt eine Postkarte an seine Freundin. Damit kein anderer sie lesen kann, benutzt er eine Geheimschrift. Entziffere die Schrift und schreibe die Karte auf einem extra Blatt neu.

DEARJANET,
I'MHEREINDENMARKWITHMYPARENTS.EVERYTHINGISAWFUL.YESTER-DAYWEWENTTOTHEBEACH,BUTITSTARTEDTORAIN.MYSTUPIDLITTLEBRO-THERALWAYSWANTSTOPLAYWITHME.HOLIDAYSWITHMYPAREN TSAREREALLYBORING.IMISSYOU.LOVE,ALEX

2 Airport

Das Datum von heute ____________

Matching: signs and words, words and sentences

Schau dir die Schilder an und verbinde sie mit den richtigen Begriffen.

handicapped facilities
ice-cream first aid car rental
tickets taxi wet floor
lift toilets no mobiles airport
no smoking information
check-in restaurant
baggage inspection no photos bus
meeting point telephones
lost-and-found train
escalator down

Wo muss Tom hin?
Lies die Sätze durch und setze die richtigen Wörter ein.

a) He wants to go by car to the next city. → ____________________

b) He wants to fly away on holiday so he goes here.

→ ____________________

c) He wants to go to the next city very fast but he doesn't want to drive.

→ ______________________________

d) He is hungry. → ______________________________

e) He wants to meet his friends. → ______________________________

f) He has hurt his head. → ______________________________

g) He wants to phone his friend and he has not got a mobile phone.

→ ______________________________

h) He wants to take the next plane so he shows his ticket here and hands in his bags. → ______________________________

i) He has lost his umbrella. → ______________________________

j) Tom's uncle cannot walk. He is in a wheelchair so Tom is happy about this.

→ ______________________________

k) He wants to go downstairs but doesn't want to wait for the lift.

→ ______________________________

l) He wants to buy a ticket. → ______________________________

a) 9th letter ___ b) 16th letter ___ c) 1st letter ___ d) 3rd letter ___

e) 9th letter ___ f) 1st letter ___ g) 5th letter ___ h) 3rd letter ___

i) 9th letter ___ j) 8th letter ___ k) 5th letter ___ l) 5th letter ___

Lösungssatz:

There are ___ ___ ___ ___ ___ ___ ___ ___ ___ ___ ___ ___ in airports.

3 Back to school

Das Datum von heute ______________

School bag, timetable, classroom phrases

Katie will ihre Schultasche packen, aber ihr Bruder hat ihre Sachen versteckt. Hilf Katie beim Suchen.

folder – cartridges – ruler – pencil case – exercise book – English book – glue – scissors

Her ______________ (Federmäppchen) is under her bed. The __________ (Hefter) and the ________ (Lineal) are in the basket. There are three ______________ (Patronen) behind the lamp on the desk. Her ________ (Klebstoff) and the ______________ (Schere) are on the bookshelf. Katie's ______________ __________ (Heft) is under the desk. Oh no, her ______________ (Englisch-) __________ (buch) is behind the cupboard.

Hier ist Katies Stundenplan. Mache einen *timetable* daraus, indem du die Fächerbezeichnungen übersetzt.

	Monday	Tuesday	Wednesday	Thursday	Friday
1st	(Englisch)	(Biologie)	(Englisch)	(Mathe)	(Sport)
2nd	(Englisch)	(Französisch)	(Französisch)	(Mathe)	(Musik)
3rd	(Geografie)	(Mathe)	(Geografie)	(Biologie)	(Englisch)
4th	(Mathe)	(Englisch)	(Geografie)	(Geschichte)	(Biologie)
5th	(Kunst)	(Sport)	(Mathe)	(Englisch)	(Französisch)
6th	(Musik)	(Sport)	(Kunst)	(Französisch)	(Geschichte)
Clubs	(Basketball)	(Hockey)	(Fußball)	(Volleyball)	

Ihr habt einen neuen Schüler in der Klasse, der noch nicht so gut Englisch spricht. Hilf ihm zu verstehen, was im Klassenraum gesagt wird. Ordne die richtigen Sätze zu.

Füllt bitte diesen Fragebogen aus.
Geht durch den Klassenraum und befragt die anderen Schüler.
Bringt bitte ein paar Fotos für euer Poster mit zur Schule.
Seid ihr fertig? Dann korrigiert bitte eure Fehler.
Könnten wir nicht dieses Foto hierhin kleben?
Lasst es uns im Uhrzeigersinn machen.

Please bring some photos for your poster to school.

____

Let's do it clockwise.

____

Walk around the classroom and ask the other pupils.

____

Couldn't we stick this photo here?

____

Fill in this questionnaire, please.

____

Have you finished? Then correct your mistakes, please.

____

4 Countries

Das Datum von heute ____________

Countries; points of the compass; geography

Schreibe die Namen der Länder auf die Karte.

Austria, Belgium, Cyprus, Denmark, England, Finland, Germany, Greece, France, Hungary, Ireland, Italy, Norway, Poland, Russian Federation, Scotland, Spain, Sweden, Switzerland, The Netherlands, Wales

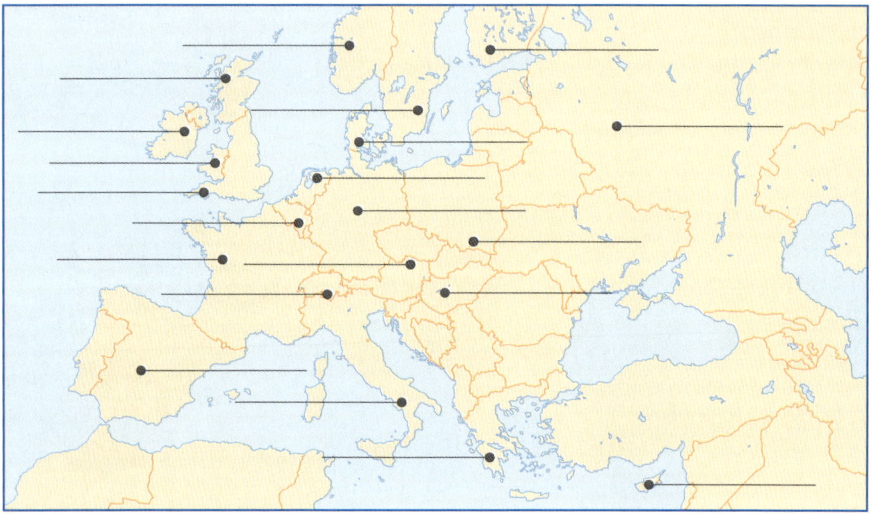

Wo sind diese Länder von dir (in Deutschland) aus gesehen auf dem Kompass zu finden?

a) Poland is in the ____________

b) Italy* is in the ____________

c) Denmark is in the ____________

d) Spain is in the ____________

e) Greece is in the ____________

f) Switzerland is in the ____________

g) Belgium** is in the ____________

* *Italy* = Italien, ** *Belgium* = Belgien

Lies die Information. Welcher Ort ist jeweils gemeint? Schreibe ihn auf.

a) This is a city in the centre of England. It has two football teams, City and United. That is ________________________. (1st letter) b) The German name is "East Sea". That is the ________________________. (9th letter) c) It is the name of the mountains in Switzerland. Those are the ______________. (3rd letter) d) You can see the Golden Gate Bridge in this city. That is ________________________. (12th letter) e) You can go to Disneyworld here. That is ___________________. (1st letter) f) The capital of this country is Canberra. That is ______________. (4th letter) g) This is the English name for München. That is ______________. (6th letter) h) The capital of this country is Reykjavik. That is _____________. (3rd letter) i) The capital of this country is Oslo. That is ______________. (4th letter) j) Germany is part of this continent. That is ___________________. (4th letter) k) This is the capital of Belgium. That is _______________________. (2nd letter) l) This is north-west of Canada. That is ___________________. (2nd letter) m) This is the capital of Scotland. That is _____________________. (2nd letter)

Lösungssatz:

A ___ ___ ___   ___ ___   ___ ___ ___   ___ ___ ___ ___ ___

makes this exercise easy.

5 Around the town

Das Datum von heute

Sounds and prepositions

Übersetze die Wörter mündlich; dann entscheide, auf welche Seite sie passen: Reimen sie sich mit *house* oder nicht?

Astronaut – August – braun – Bluse – fand – Gruppe – hinunter – jetzt – Kuh – Land – laut – Stunde – Tor – Wellensittich – wie – zählen – zeichnen – Schule – Laden – Tisch

Sounds like: *house*	**Doesn't sound like: *house***

ie oder *ei*

Alle Wörter werden mit *ie* geschrieben, bis auf zwei.
Sie werden mit *ei* geschrieben. Welche?

bel ______ ve, l ______, n ______ ghbour, budg ______,

pat ______ nt, d ______, fr ______ nd, interv ______ w, p ______ ce,

qu ______ t, sc ______ nce, f ______ ld, old ______, ______ ther

Schreibe die fehlenden Wörter in die Lücken.
Schau dir dafür die Straße an:
opposite – in front of – next to – between – behind

1. The post office is opposite the swimming pool. 2. The swimming pool is ________________ the hotel. 3. The café is ____________________ the hotel and the supermarket. 4. The pet shop is ____________________ the church and the school and ____________________ the café. 5. The supermarket is ________________________ house number 8. 6. House number 4 is _____________________ house number 2 and _____________________ the hotel. 7. The snack bar is ________________ the church. 8. House number 10 is ____________________ the hospital and _______________ house number 8. 9. The hotel is ____________________ the café and the swimming pool and _______________________ house number 4 and __________________ the school. 10. The school is ____.

(Hier kannst du so viel schreiben, wie du möchtest.)

6 Asking and telling the way

Das Datum von heute ____________

A computer game

Paula spielt ein Computerspiel, bei dem sie einen Schatz sucht. Dazu muss sie drei Fragen entschlüsseln und dann die richtigen Antworten anklicken.

me | Excuse | , | please | . | ______________________________

the | Treasure | you | to | tell | way | Island | me | Can | ? |

____

do | I | the | How | to | get | castle | ? | ______________________________

is | of | gold | the | Where | bag | ? | ______________________________

Welcome to Treasure Island! You want to find a bag of gold?
Then follow the instructions. You are in front of the „Sunshine Hotel".

1. ☐ (P) Between / ☐ (S) Next to / ☐ (T) On top of the hotel there is 2. ☐ (W) the car park. / ☐ (T) the swimming pool. / ☐ (A) the bank. When you leave the hotel you must 3. ☐ (B) go straight on / ☐ (N) turn left / ☐ (R) turn right to come to the camp-site. The camp-site is 4. ☐ (E) between / ☐ (A) in front of / ☐ (O) next to the zoo and the lake. When you are in front of the camp-site, 5. ☐ (K) walk down / ☐ (E) turn left / ☐ (H) turn right into Pool Street and then 6. ☐ (T) go straight on / ☐ (B) take the first street on the right / ☐ (L) turn left until you come to a very big tree. The tree is in a wonderful park. Go 7. ☐ (Z) up / ☐ (G) over / ☐ (P) through the park. In the park there is a 8. ☐ (L) visitor centre / ☐ (F) school / ☐ (C) bank where you can get a lot of information about Treasure Island. Don't miss it. 9. ☐ (D) On top of / ☐ (A) Behind / ☐ (S) Between the visitor centre there is a little café. Leave the park through the north gate. 10. ☐ (N) Walk up / ☐ (V) Cross / ☐ (J) Turn right into High Street for 100 metres. Take the third street on the right. Behind the castle you will find the bag of gold in the garden under a big stone.

Trage die Lösungsbuchstaben hier ein und du erhältst den Lösungssatz:

A ___ ___ ___ ___ ___ ___ ___ ___ ___ ___ **can help you to find your way.**
(1 2 3 4 5 6 7 8 9 10)

7 Traffic

Das Datum von heute

Traffic signs; a crossword puzzle

Nick lernt für eine Fahrradprüfung. Dazu hat er sich die Bedeutung der Verkehrszeichen auf Karteikarten geschrieben. Ordne die Bezeichnungen von S. 19 den richtigen Karteikarten zu.

Fire department	Police	Hostel
Speed limit	Footpath	School
No overtaking	Road narrows	No parking
Uneven road	Crossroads	Priority road
No bicycles	No stopping	No parking
Traffic signals ahead	Bicycle lane/path	No entry
Dead end	Camping	Crosswind
Go to the right	Expressway	Hospital

Es bleiben sechs Kärtchen übrig. Mit deren Hilfe kannst du das kleine Kreuzworträtsel lösen. Wie heißt das Lösungswort?

BIKE

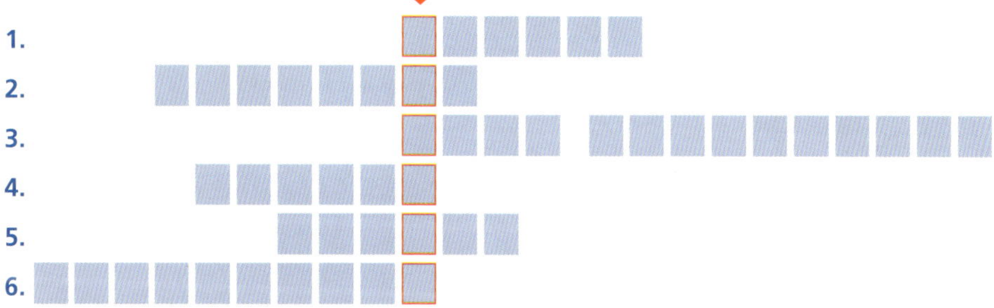

IS IMPORTANT FOR YOU.

1. Children go there to learn something.
2. You have got a broken arm. You must go to ...
3. You find a lot fire engines here.
4. You call them when there is an accident in the street.
5. Young people stay here when they are on holiday.
6. It is a road where cars can go very fast.

8 Quantities

Das Datum von heute ______

Containers and food

Benenne die Gegenstände.

bottle – box – bag – packet – tin – piece – plate – jar – glass

______ ______ ______

______ ______ ______

 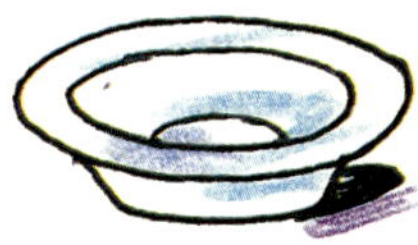 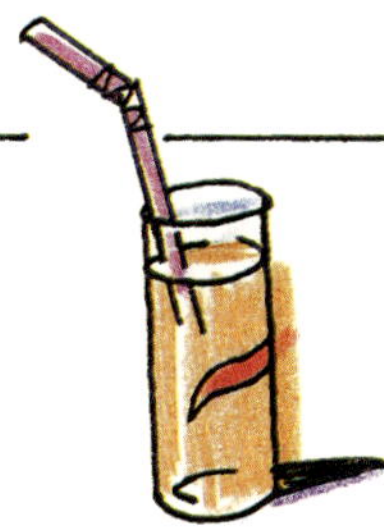

______ ______ ______

Ziehe jeweils einen Strich zum Lebensmittel.

a bottle of

a plate of

Übersetze die unterstrichenen Teile:

a) Zum Frühstück esse ich immer eine Scheibe Brot und trinke ein Glas Milch.

b) Ich kaufe eine Flasche Cola. c) Reiche mir bitte die Cornflakes-Packung.

d) Ich habe eine Schachtel Schokokekse gekauft. e) Colin hat das Glas Erdnussbutter fallen lassen. f) Mary kaufte eine Dose Fisch.

a) ______________________ d) ______________________

b) ______________________ e) ______________________

c) ______________________ f) ______________________

9 Parties

Das Datum von heute

Different parties; Invitations

January	February	March	April	May	June
Peter's birthday	Fancy dress party	Birthday grandma	Fool's day party	My 12th birthday	Garden party at the Millers'
July	**August**	**September**	**October**	**November**	**December**
School party	Garden party with the neigh-bours	Fancy dress party in the tennis club	Halloween	Bonfire night	Boxing Day Party New Year's party

Wie heißt die Party, zu der du deine Freunde einlädst?

a) You like pumkins, ghosts and scary clothes. → ______________________

b) You celebrate it on the 26th December. → ______________________

c) At the end of term the pupils are happy that school is over. → ______________________

d) Now you are 12 years old. → ______________________

e) It's on the 31st December. → ______________________

f) The weather is fine. You don't want to have a party in the house. → ______________________

g) People celebrate it on the 5th November, because Guy Fawkes didn't blow up the king and the Parliament. → ______________________

h) You like to wear funny or crazy clothes. → ______________________

23 Schreibe für drei verschiedene Partys die passenden Einladungskarten.

Birthday party

Dear John,

____

____

____

Bonfire night party

Dear Daisy,

____

____

____

Garden party

Dear Peter,

____

____

____

Come to our house on 22nd July at 5 o'clock.

The party is on 5th November at 19.00.

The party is on 23rd January at 3 o'clock.

Do you like bonfires?

I'll be 13 next month. I want to invite you.

Do you want to have a great barbecue?

Please bring your own fireworks.

We can dance in our party room.

Hope the weather will be fine.

10 Bonfire night

Das Datum von heute

____

Crossword puzzle; Guy Fawkes' story

Across: →

2. Hähnchenbein
9. Salat
10. gefährlich
12. Feuer
16. fernhalten von
17. Würstchen
18. Pommes
19. Krankenhaus

Down: ↓

1. zurücktreten
3. Parlamentsgebäude
4. essen
5. Butterbrote
6. Wort für ein lautes Geräusch
7. obendrauf
8. November
11. Feuerwerk, Feuerwerkskörper
15. Kartoffelchips
16. König
13. Wer wollte das Parlament in die Luft sprengen?
14. Limonade

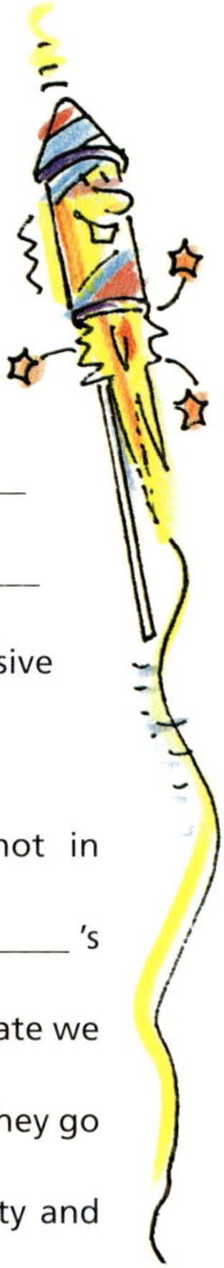

Benutze einige Wörter aus dem Kreuzworträtsel, um die Lücken auszufüllen.
Tipp: Manche Wörter kommen mehrmals vor.

__________ __________ didn't like the __________

so he wanted to __________ ______ the __________

______ ____________________ with lots of explosive

gunpowder. He went under the __________ ______

____________________ with his men. That was not in

September, it was in ______________. But the __________'s

men knew about his plan so they caught him. Now, every year to celebrate we

make a big __________ with lots of noisy __________ – they go

__________ !!! and fly up in the sky. Sometimes we have a party and

invite all our friends. We eat __________ ______, __________,

and __________ and we drink __________. My parents say that

__________ are very __________.

11 Ready for a meal

Das Datum von heute ____________

Difficult words; a code puzzle

Schreibe *make* oder *do* in die Lücken.

a) ______________ the bed

b) ______________ a cake

c) ______________ notes

d) ______________ the dishes

e) ______________ a trip

f) ______________ a job

g) ______________ my homework

h) ______________ exercise number 10

i) ______________ music

j) ______________ a noise

l) ______________ a crossword puzzle

m) ______________ the dinner

n) ______________ the shopping

Wie viele Male hast du *make* benutzt? Und *do*?

make = ___ *do* = ___

Versuche dieses Rätsel zu lösen. Es hilft, wenn du alle gleichen Zahlen mit den zugeordneten Buchstaben ausfüllst.

A	B	C	D	E	F	G	H	I	J	K	L	M

N	O	P	Q	R	S	T	U	V	W	X	Y	Z
											5	

___ O ___ // ___ A ___ ___ // ___ ___ // ___ ___ ___ // ___ ___ ___ // ___ ___ ___ ___ ___ ___ //
5 21 1 — 12 23 18 22 — 8 21 — 16 1 8 — 8 12 22 — 7 25 3 12 22 3

___ ___ // ___ ___ ___ // ___ ___ ___ ___ ___ // B ___ ___ ___ ___ ___ // ___ // ___ ___ ___ ___ //
21 9 — 8 12 22 — 8 23 11 19 22 — 11 22 2 21 13 22 — 23 — 6 22 23 19

___ ___ ___ // ___ ___ ___ ___ R // ___ ___ ___ // ___ ___ ___ ___ // ___ ___ ___ // ___ ___ ___ ___ //
23 9 7 — 23 2 8 22 13 — 8 12 22 — 6 22 23 19 — 5 21 1 — 12 23 18 22

___ ___ // ___ ___ ___ ___ // ___ ___ ___ // ___ ___ S ___ ___ ___.
8 21 — 10 23 3 12 — 8 12 22 — 7 25 3 12 22 3

12 Jobs in the house

Das Datum von heute ____________

Verb phrases

	Monday	Tuesday	Wednesday	Thursday	Friday	Saturday
	mum/dad	mum	mum	mum	mum	mum/dad
	dad	mum	dad	dad	mum	dad
	Peter	Molly	Peter	Molly	Peter	Molly
	mum	mum	mum	mum	mum	everyone
	Molly	Molly	Molly	Molly	Molly	Peter
	Peter	Molly	dad	Peter	Molly	dad

a) Schau dir die Tabelle an. Sage, was wer macht.

1. Monday  ____________

2. Wednesday  ____________

3. Tuesday  ____________

4. Saturday  ____________

b) Benutze eines der folgenden Wörter und schreibe in die Sätze, wie häufig jemand etwas tut.

often – never – sometimes – usually

5. (go shopping) Mum ______________________________.

6. (make breakfast) Peter ______________________________.

7. (make the beds) Mum ______________________________.

8. (take the rubbish out) Mum ______________________________.

9. (wash the dishes) Molly ______________________________.

10. (feed the cat) Molly ______________________________.

Finde heraus, was diese Kinder zu Hause für Aufgaben haben.

1	2 ABC	3 DEF
4 GHI	5 JKL	6 MNO
7 PQRS	8 TUV	9 WXYZ
*	0 +	#

____

Paul: 3 3 3 3 8 4 3 3 6 4

____

Jenny: 2 8 9 8 4 3 6 3 9 7 7 2 7 3 7

____

Peter: 8 4 3 9 8 7 8 4 3 5 4 8 2 4 3 6

____

Meg: 6 2 5 3 8 4 3 2 3 3 7

____

Diana: 2 6 6 5 3 4 6 6 3 7

13 Keeping a pet

Das Datum von heute ____________

Grouping words; words with double letters

Streiche alle Körperteile durch. Dann: alle Tiere, die Beine haben, alles was du essen oder trinken kannst. Zum Schluss alles, was du auf der Straße sehen kannst. Schreibe die übrigen Wörter unten auf.

hip	A	fruit	traffic	goldfish	juice
is	cat	budgie	apple	cake	very
ear	cocoa	boring	face	spider	church
It	swims	bone	shop	neck	around
pavement	toes	all	ambulance	day	car

Lösungssatz: A _.

It _.

Fische die fehlenden Buchstaben aus dem richtigen Becken und schreibe die vervollständigten Wörter von S. 31 in alphabetisher Reihenfolge darunter.

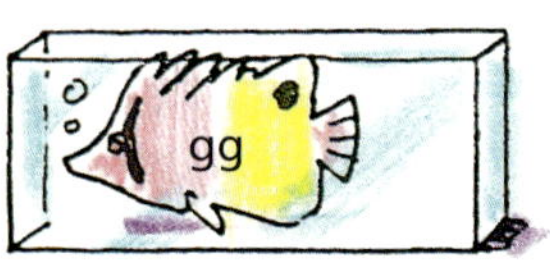

aftern______n // a______ear // be______er // bi______er // blo______om // bri______iant // cart______n // ca______ette // ch______se // di______erent // di______er // e______s // fe______y // fo______y // fu______y // gira______e // gue______ // ha______y // ho______ible // la______er // le______uce // o______ice // o______osite // pre______y // po______ute // pu______ing // ra______it // r______m // ru______er // ru______ish // str______t // su______enly // su______y // tomo______ow // usua______y // w______kend

14 The weather

Das Datum von heute

Weather station, weather forecast

Ordne die Wetteradjektive der richtigen Seite der Wetterstation zu.

beautiful – bad – terrible – nice – warm – sunny – awful – cloudy – brilliant – cold – great – windy – stormy – fine – wonderful – foggy – good – dark – rainy – hot

Lösungen

1

1. go skiing
2. go hiking
3. go on a bike trip
4. go swimming and sailing
5. take photos
6. go on a safari and see an elefant
7. go surfing
8. go camping

a) Campsite; **b)** youth hostel; **c)** holiday apartment; **d)** farm; **e)** house boat; **f)** hotels

Dear Janet,
I'm here in Denmark with my parents. Everything is awful. Yesterday we went to the beach, but it started to rain. My stupid little brother always wants to play with me. Holidays with my parents are really boring. I miss you.
Love, Alex

2

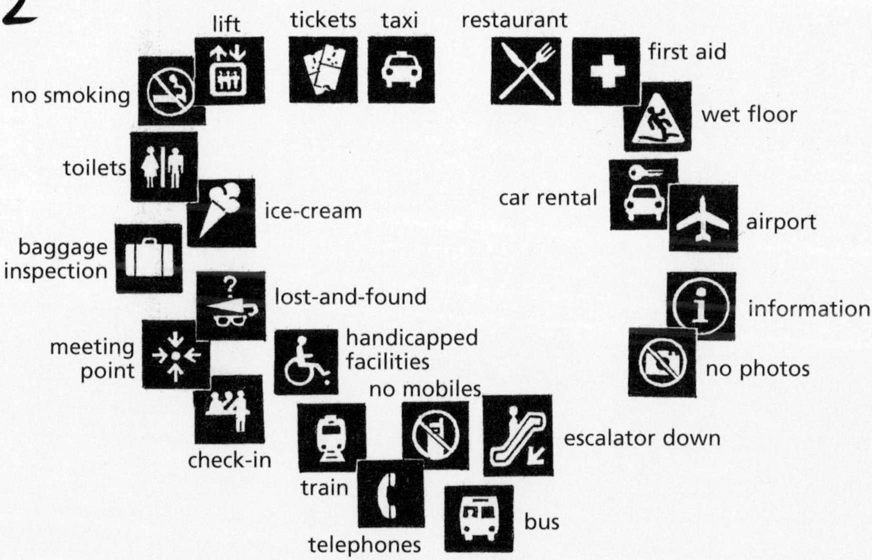

a) car rental; **b)** baggage inspection; **c)** train; **d)** restaurant; **e)** meeting point; **f)** first aid; **g)** telephones; **h)** check-in; **i)** lost-and-found; **j)** handicapped facilities; **k)** escalator down; **l)** tickets

a) L; **b)** O; **c)** T; **d)** S; **e)** O; **f)** F; **g)** P; **h)** E; **i)** O; **j)** P; **k)** L; **l)** E
Lösungssatz: There are **lots of people** in airports.

3

pencil case – folder – ruler – cartridges – glue – scissors – exercise book – English book

Englisch – English, Geografie – geography, Mathe(matik) – math(ematic)s, Kunst – art, Biologie – biology, Französisch – French, Geschichte – history, Musik – music, Basketball – basket ball, Hockey – hockey, Fußball – football, Volleyball – volleyball

Bringt bitte ein paar Fotos für euer Poster mit zur Schule. – Lasst es uns im Uhrzeigersinn machen. – Geht durch den Klassenraum und befragt die anderen Schüler. – Könnten wir nicht dieses Foto hierhin kleben? – Füllt bitte diesen Fragebogen aus. – Seid ihr fertig? Dann korrigiert bitte eure Fehler.

4

a) east; **b)** south; **c)** north; **d)** south-west; **e)** south-east; **f)** south-west; **g)** west

a) Manchester; **b)** Baltic Sea; **c)** the Alps; **d)** San Francisco; **e)** Florida; **f)** Australia; **g)** Munich; **h)** Iceland; **i)** Norway; **j)** Europe; **k)** Brussels; **l)** Alaska; **m)** Edingburgh

Lösungssatz: A **map of the world** makes this exercise easy.

5

(links:) brown, blouse, found, down, now, cow, loud, hour, how, count
(rechts:) astronaut, August, country, group, gate, budgie, draw, school, shop, table

believe; lie; neighbour; budgie; patient; die; friend; interview; piece; quiet; science; field; oldie; either

2. next to; **3.** between; **4.** between, opposite; **5.** opposite; **6.** next to, behind; **7.** next to; **8.** opposite, next to; **9.** between, opposite, opposite;

6

Excuse me, please.
Can you tell me the way to Treasure Island?
How do I get to the castle?
Where ist the bag of gold?

Lösungssatz: A **street plan** can help you to find your way.

7

Traffic signals ahead

Speed limit

Priority road

Road narrows

Crossroads

No overtaking

No entry

Roundabout

Uneven road

No bicycles

No stopping

No parking

Bicycle lane/path

Footpath

Go to the right

Dead end

Camping

Crosswind

BIKE ↓

1. SCHOOL
2. HOSPITAL
3. FIRE DEPARTMENT
4. POLICE
5. HOSTEL
6. EXPRESSWAY

→ IS IMPORTANT FOR YOU.

8

jar, piece, packet
box, (tea) bag, bottle
tin, plate, glass

a bottle of milk 

a plate of soup 

a bag of apples 

a tin of fish 

a jar of marmalade 

a box of chocolates 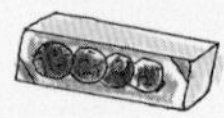

a glass of coke 

a piece of bread 

a) a piece of bread, a glass of milk; **b)** a bottle of coke; **c)** the packet of cornflakes; **d)** a box of chocolates; **e)** the jar of peanut butter; **f)** a tin of fish

9

a) A Halloween party; **b)** Boxing Day; **c)** School party; **d)** My birthday party; **e)** New year's party; **f)** A garden party with the neighbours; **g)** Bonfire night; **h)** Fancy dress party in the tennis club

Birthday party
Dear John,
I'll be 13 next month. I want to invite you. The party is on 23rd January at 3 o'clock.
We can dance in our party room.

Bonfire night party
Dear Daisy,
Do you like bonfires? The party is on 5th November at 19.00.
Please bring your own fireworks.

Garden party
Dear Peter,
Do you want to have a great barbecue?
Come to our house on 22nd July at 5 o'clock. Hope the weather will be fine.

10

1 S			2 C	3 H	I	C	K	4 E	N	L	E	G	5 S
T				O				A					A
A				U				T		6 B			N
N		7 O		S		8 N			9 S	A	L	A	D
10 D	A	N	G	E	R	O	U	S		N			W
B		T		S		V				G			I
A		O		O		E							C
C		P		F		M			11 F				H
K		O		P		B		12 F	I	R	E		E
		F		A		E			R				S
				R		R			E				
				L			13 G		W				
		14 L		I			U		O				15 C
16 K	E	E	P	A	W	A	Y	F	R	O	M		R
I		M		M			F		K				I
N		O		E		17 S	A	U	S	A	G	E	S
G		N		N			W						P
		A		T			K		18 C	H	I	P	S
		D					E						
		E			19 H	O	S	P	I	T	A	L	

Guy Fawkes – king – blow up – Houses of Parliament – Houses of Parliament – November – king – fire – fireworks – bang – chicken legs – chips – crisps – lemonade – fireworks – dangerous

11

a) make the bed; **b)** make a cake; **c)** make notes; **d)** do the dishes; **e)** make a trip; **f)** do a job; **g)** do my homework; **h)** do exercise number 10; **i)** make music; **j)** make a noise; **l)** do a crossword puzzle; **m)** make the dinner; **n)** do the shopping

make: 7-mal; do: 6-mal

Lösungssatz:
You have to put the dishes on the table before a meal and after the meal you have to wash the dishes.

12

a)
1. (On Mondays,) Peter washes the dishes. **3.** (On Tuesdays,) mum makes breakfast.
2. (On Wednesdays,) mum goes shopping. **4.** (On Saturdays,) dad takes out the rubbish.

b)
5. Mum often goes shopping. **6.** Peter never makes breakfast. **7.** Mum usually makes the beds. **8.** Mum never takes the rubbish out. **9.** Molly sometimes washes the dishes. **10.** Molly usually feeds the cat.

Paul: feed the dog; Jenny: buy the newspaper; Peter: tidy up the kitchen; Meg: make the beds; Diana: cook dinner

13

Streichen:
Köperteile: hip, ear, toes, bone, face, neck;
Tiere, die Beine haben: cat, budgie, spider;
zu essen/trinken: cocoa, fruit, apple, cake, juice;
auf der Straße zu sehen: pavement, traffic, shop, ambulance, church, car

Lösungssatz:
A goldfish is very boring. It swims around all day.

afternoon // appear // better // bigger // blossom // brilliant // cartoon // cassette // cheese // different // dinner // eggs // ferry // foggy // fully // giraffe // guess // happy // horrible // ladder // lettuce // office // opposite // pretty // pollute // pudding // rabbit // room // runner // rubbish // street // suddenly // sunny // tomorrow // usually // weekend

14

bad, terrible, awful, cloudy, cold, windy, stormy, foggy, dark, rainy

beautiful, nice, warm, sunny, brilliant, great, fine, wonderful, good, hot

Text:
Good evening ladies and gentlemen,
Here is the latest weather forecast for Great Britain.
Yesterday it was sunny and quite warm. But today there will only be sunshine in the morning. In the afternoon there will be some clouds in the sky and perhaps it will start to rain.
Tomorrow we expect terrible weather. It will be very cold, perhaps there will be ice on the roads. In Scotland and Wales you will find good skiing conditions.
In the London area it will be foggy and rainy.

Lösungssatz: Don't go outside. There will be a hurricane tonight.

15

a) English; **b)** maths; **c)** history; **d)** geography; **e)** music; **f)** French; **g)** art

a) behind; **b)** in front of; **c)** next to; **d)** between; **e)** opposite

a) no overtaking; **b)** traffic lights; **c)** no parking; **d)** bicycle path/lane

a) bottle of milk; **b)** bag of peanuts; **c)** piece of cake; **d)** tin of fish; **e)** cup of tea

16

1. Fülle die Bisquits in die große Schüssel. **2.** Öffne die Obstkonservendose. **3.** Gib Früchte und Fruchtsaft auf die Bisquits. **4.** Mache die Götterspeise: Fülle (1/2 l) Wasser und den Inhalt der Packung Götterspeise in einen Topf. Sehr stark erhitzen. Fünf Minuten warten, dann die Götterspeise auf die Früchte in der großen Schüssel geben. Warte 20 Minuten, bis die Götterspeise fest wird. **5.** Mache den Vanillepudding. Fülle (1/2 l) Milch in eine Schüssel. Gib das Puddingpulver und etwas Zucker dazu und rühre alles gut mit dem Schneebesen durch. Fülle die Masse auf die Götterspeise. **6.** Gib die Sahne in eine Schüssel und schlage sie mit dem Schneebesen (oder einem elektrischen Mixer) steif. **7.** Fülle die Sahne auf den Vanillepudding. **8.** Dekoriere das Ganze mit Smarties und Gummibärchen. **9.** Lade deine Familie ein und – genießt!

2. cat; **3.** tea; **4.** car; **5.** cap; **6.** cut

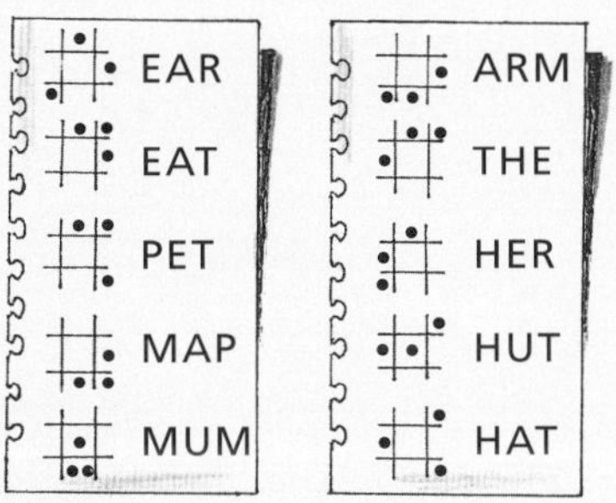

17

Lösungssatz: Giggi knows a **lot of nice girls**. But at the moment he is **single**.

You are like a tear in my eye. / I will never cry / because then / would lose you.
You are like the air in my lungs. / I will never breathe out / because then I would lose you.
You are like the hair on my head. / I will never cut it / because then I would lose you.
You are like a dream at night. / I will never wake up / because then I would lose you.
You are like the sun in the sky. / I hope it will never go down / because then I would lose you.

Es gibt 43 "to" in dem Song.

18

☆ red, yellow, blue, green, brown, black, white

☆☆

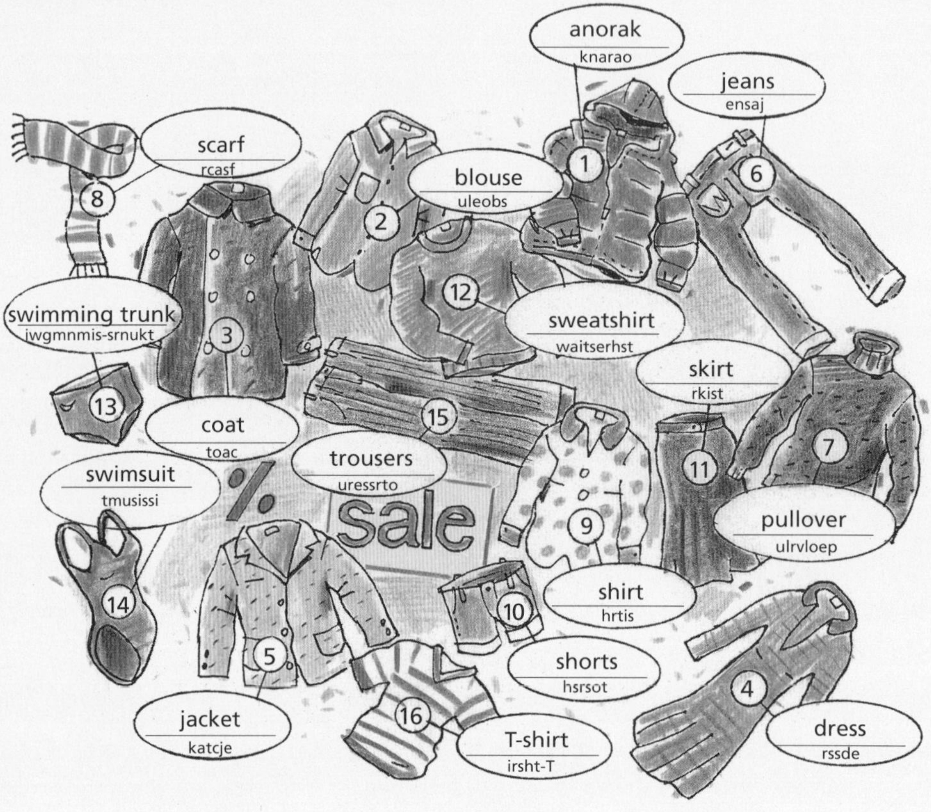

☆☆☆ Hello, I'm looking for a new school uniform. – I need a grey skirt, a blue blazer, a black pullover and a white blouse. – I think size 12 is okay. – Yes, it's fine. Now, where do I find skirts? – How does this skirt look on me? – Okay, I'll take the blazer, the grey skirt and two white blouses. – How much is this black pullover? – Can I try it on? – Okay, I'll take it, too. Thank you for your help.

19

☆

frame	1	12	Gabel
saddle	2	3	Lenker
handlebar	3	7	Vorderlicht
front brake	4	9	Reifen
back brake	5	13	Speiche
flag	6	1	Rahmen
front light	7	11	Pedale
rear light	8	5	Rückbremse
tyre	9	14	Schutzblech
rain jacket	10	2	Sattel
pedals	11	6	Fahne
fork	12	20	Gangschaltung
spoke	13	4	Vorderbremse
mudguard	14	8	Rücklicht
reflectors	15	17	Klingel
basket	16	19	Schloss
bell	17	10	Regenjacke
chain	18	18	Kette
lock	19	16	Korb
gear shift	20	15	Reflektoren

Lösungssatz: You must **always wear** a **bike helmet**.

☆☆ flag, rain jacket, mudguard, basket, lock, gear shift

a) Always keep your eyes open.
b) Turn your lights on at night.
c) Use a bike path.
d) Don't ride the wrong way in a street.
e) Don't ride on the pavement.
f) Wear bright clothes so that drivers can see you.

20

☆

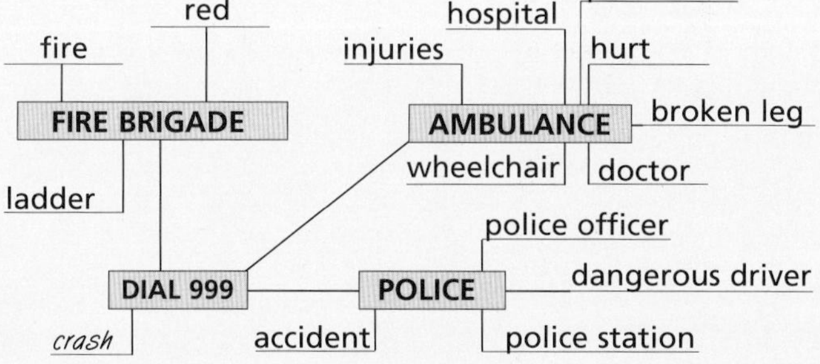

a) of; **b)** up; **c)** for; **d)** into; **e)** across; **f)** about

Mögliche Lösungen sind:
1. I fell off a ladder and now I have got backache. **2.** I had a bike accident and now I have head injuries. **3.** I played golf and a ball hit my eye. **4.** An elephant stood on my toe and now it is broken. **5.** I hit my finger with a hammer and now it really hurts. **6.** I had a car accident and now I have to wear a neck bandage. **7.** I fell and now my arm is in a sling. **8.** I played football and now my broken leg is in plaster (= in Gips).

21

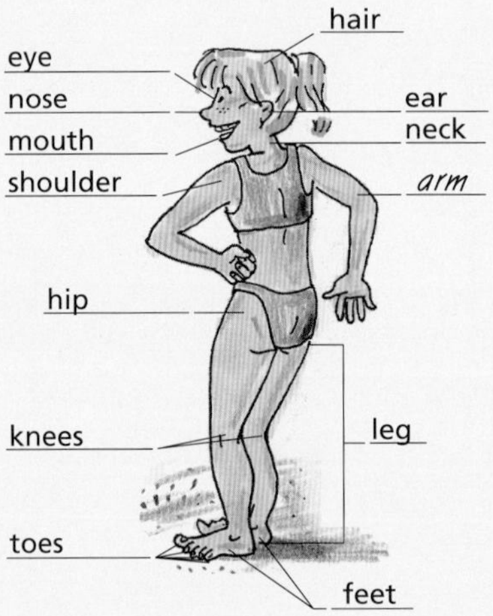

a) legs–ears–head–eyes; **b)** neck–legs; **c)** legs–feet; **d)** arms; **e)** ears; **f)** legs–teeth–mouth; **g)** legs–eyes–body; **h)** legs–teeth–mouth; **i)** body–legs; **j)** legs–neck–eyes

22

Lösungssatz: Welcome to the 'Funny People's Club', Mr **Wonderful**!

1. Mr Botter **2.** Mr Brown **3.** Mr Benson **4.** Mr Barker

23

at the moment – at once – at home – at night –at six o'clock – in English – in 1654 – in the country – in the morning – on the photo – in the street – on the beach – on 12th July – on the bus – at (=am)/on (=auf dem) the table – on TV – on Monday – for tea – for example – for a long time – for weeks

Aktivität/Tätigkeit – activity; Farbe – colour; Filzstift – felt tip; hübsch – nice; Karte – card; Karton – cardboard; Klebstoff – glue; Kostüm – costume; Lineal – ruler; machen – do; Material – material; Papier – paper; Foto – photo; Fotoapparat – camera; Pinsel –

brush; Plastik – plastic; Schere – scissors; schön – beautiful; Stück – piece; trocken – dry; vollständig – complete; wunderbar – wonderful; zeichnen – draw

Lösungssatz: If you want to make a card for somebody you need cardboard, felt tips, scissors, glue and a good idea.

24

Infinitive	Simple past	Past participle	German
be	was / were	been	sein
buy	bought	bought	kaufen
come	came	come	kommen
do	did	done	tun
drink	drank	drunk	trinken
eat	ate	eaten	essen
give	gave	given	geben
go	went	gone	gehen
have	had	had	haben
make	made	made	machen
meet	met	met	treffen
pay	paid	paid	bezahlen
read	read	read	lesen
run	ran	run	rennen
say	said	said	sagen
see	saw	seen	sehen
sleep	slept	slept	schlafen
take	took	taken	nehmen
understand	understood	understood	verstehen
write	wrote	written	schreiben

25

2. river – **6.** barbecue – **4.** park – picnic – **9.** – **1.** bike – **5.** lake – rowing boats – island – **7.** – **3.** village – **10.** – **8.**

We rode along a river on a nice bike path. – We saw a nice village with a little harbour. – At lunchtime we stopped in a park where we had a picnic. – In the park there was a lake. Near a café we saw a sign: "Rowing boats for rent." In the middle of the lake there was a small island. – We left our bikes near the café and rowed to the little island where we had a barbecue. – In the evening we got back to the café. – Alan noticed that his bike was gone. So we went into the café. – The owner told us: "You haven't locked your bike. So I kept it in my café for you." – Before we went home, he invited us to a nice piece of strawberry cake.

26

Umwelt – environment – verschmutzen – pollute – Wiederverwertung – recycling – Sonnenenergie – solar energy – Wald – forest – saurer Regen – acid rain – Fabrik – factory – Mülltonne – bin – retten – save – Kraftwerk – power station – Altglas-Container – bottle bank

				o	c	e	a	n	w	s
		n			p				a	u
e		o			o			w	t	n
n		i		t	l			o	e	
e	r	s		r	l			r	r	b
r	i	e		e	u			l		e
g	v			e	t			d		a
y	e			s	i					c
	r			f	o	r	e	s	t	h
					n					
				g	r	o	u	n	d	

in alphabetischer Reihenfolge:
1. beach **2.** energy **3.** forest **4.** ground **5.** noise **6.** ocean **7.** pollution **8.** river **9.** sun **10.** trees **11.** water **12.** world

Lösungssatz: Save our world!

27

afternoon, basketball, bathroom, birthday, bookshelf, boyfriend, breakfast, cardboard, clockwise, cupboard, cornflakes, downstairs, everything, goldfish, homework, motorbike, newspaper, overtake, peanut, pullover, timetable, understand, walkman, wallpaper, weekend, wildlife, without, grandmother

1. before **2.** near **3.** in front of **4.** down **5.** dirty **6.** cheap **7.** dangerous **8.** different **9.** last **10.** easy **11.** happy **12.** hungry **13.** long **14.** worse **15.** small **16.** never **17.** boring **18.** wet **19.** untidy

Lösungssatz: Well done!!!!! You are great!

28

a) ~~bikini~~; **b)** ~~bikini~~ (zweiteilig) oder ~~swimming trunks~~ (für Jungs); **c)** ~~shirt~~; **d)** ~~sandals~~; **e)** ~~trousers~~

My clothes	My bike	My body
trousers coat shoes scarf jeans	handlebar frame brakes tyre pedals	toes teeth eyes leg hair

Bild (1) – Text (B); Bild (2) – Text (A); Bild (3) – Text (C)

gehen	go~~h~~	went	gone
sagen	sa~~i~~y	said	said
schreiben	write	wrote	written
lesen	read	read	read~~en~~
kaufen	buy	bought	bought

Lies dir die Wettervorhersage sorgfältig durch. Markiere alle „überflüssigen" Buchstaben und trage sie unten ein. Du erhältst eine Warnmeldung.

Goodd eveoning ladies annd gentlemten,

Here is tghe loatest weather forecast foor Greuat Britain.
Yesterday it was stunny and quitse warm. But today there will oinly be sundshine in thee mortning. Inh the aefternoon threre will be seome clouwds in the siky and lperhaps ilt will start to rain.
Tomborrow we expect tererible weaather. It will be vehry cold, peurhaps there will be ice on the roads.
In Srcotland aind Wcales you waill find gonod skiing coneditions.
Int the Loondon narea it iwill beg foggy hand raitny.

___ ___ ___ ' ___   ___ ___   ___ ___ ___ ___ ___ ___ ___.
1 2 3 4   5 6   7 8 9 10 11 12 13

___ ___ ___ ___ ___   ___ ___ ___ ___   ___ ___   ___
14 15 16 17 18   19 20 21 22   23 24   25

___ ___ ___ ___ ___ ___ ___ ___ ___   ___ ___ ___ ___ ___ ___ ___.
26 27 28 29 30 31 32 33 34   35 36 37 38 39 40 41

15 Test

Das Datum von heute

____

School subjects. Schreibe die Namen der Fächer auf.

a) This is ______________________ .

b) This is ______________________ .

c) This is ______________________ .

d) This is ______________________ .

e) This is ______________________ .

f) This is ______________________ .

g) This is ______________________ .

Für jedes richtig gefundene Wort erhältst du einen Punkt.

Ich habe ____ Punkte.

Where is the mouse? Schreibe auf, wo die Maus sich befindet.

a)

c)

e)

a) The mouse is ____________________ the cat.

b) The mouse is ____________________ the cat.

c) The mouse is ____________________ the cat.

d) The mouse is ____________________ the cats.

e) The mouse is ____________________ the cat.

b)

d)

Für jedes richtig gefundene Wort erhältst du einen Punkt.

Ich habe ____ Punkte.

Traffic signs. Trage die englischen Bedeutungen ein.

a) 

____

b) 

____

c) 

____

d) 

____

Für jedes richtig gefundene Wort erhältst du einen Punkt.

Ich habe ____ Punkte.

What are these? Schreibe auf, was auf den Bildern zu sehen ist.
Vergiss die Gefäße bzw. Behälter nicht.

a) This is a __________________________ .

b) This is a __________________________ .

c) This is a __________________________ .

d) This is a __________________________ .

e) This is a __________________________ .

Für jeden richtig gefundenen Ausdruck erhältst du einen Punkt.

Ich habe ____ Punkte.

Addiere deine Punkte aus allen vier Übungen. Ich habe ___ Punkte insgesamt.
26 Punkte: Deine Leistung ist sehr gut. Mehr als 21 Punkte: Deine Leistung ist gut. Mehr als 18 Punkte: In Ordnung! Mehr als 16 Punkte: Es könnte besser sein! Weniger als 13 Punkte: Du solltest die Kapitel 1–14 noch einmal wiederholen!

16 Take a break

Das Datum von heute

Working in the kitchen; cracking a code

Making a trifle*

Diese Geräte brauchst du:

Diese Zutaten brauchst du:

1. Put the biscuits into the bowl.

2. Open the tin of fruit.

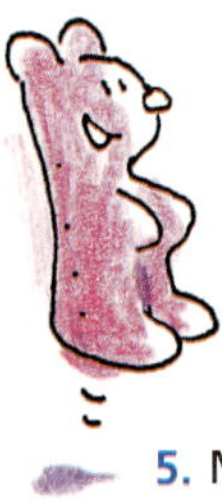

3. Put the fruit and the juice on the biscuits.

4. Make the jelly: Put the water in a pot with the packet of jelly. Make it very hot. Wait five minutes, now put the jelly onto the fruit in the bowl. Wait 20 minutes for the jelly to get hard.

5. Make the vanilla pudding. Put the milk in a bowl. Add the vanilla pudding, a little sugar and mix it well with the whisk. Put it on the jelly in the bowl.

6. Put the cream in a bowl, mix it with the whisk and make it stiff*.

7. Put the cream on the vanilla pudding.

8. Make it pretty with smarties and gummi bears!!!

9. Invite your family and ENJOY!!!

* *trifle* = Britische Spezialität: ein aus Götterspeise, Bisquit, Früchten, Vanillesoße und Sahne gemachter Nachtisch; wörtlich „eine Kleinigkeit"

* *stiff* = steif (Sahne)

Cracking the code

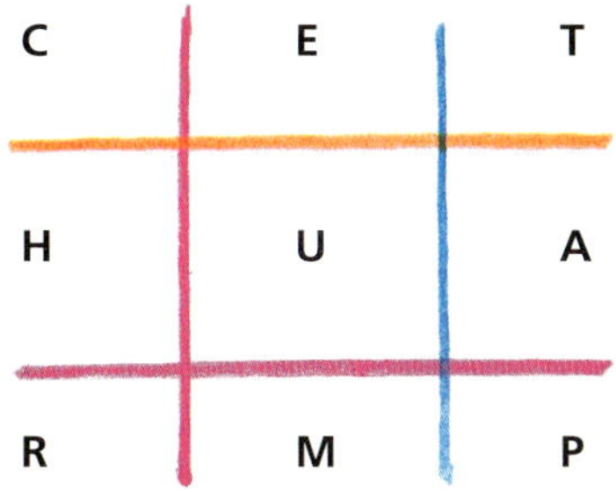

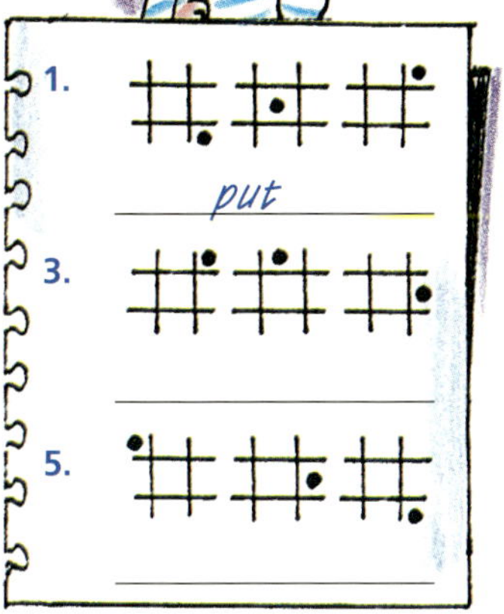

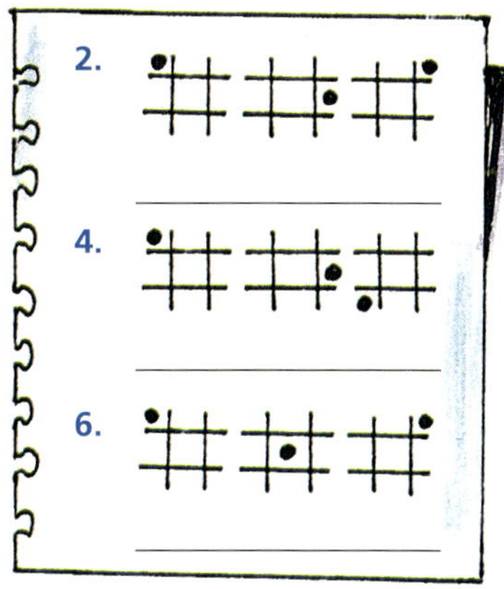

Schreibe jetzt die folgenden Wörter auf ein extra Blatt. Benutze dazu die Geheimschrift, aber diesmal alle Punkte in einem Raster.
Kann dein Freund die Wörter erraten?

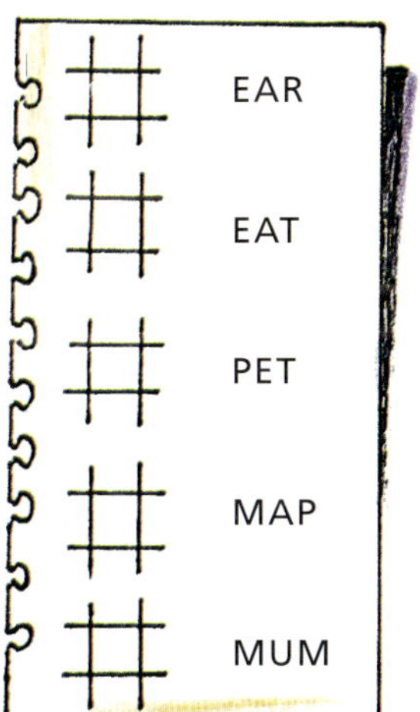

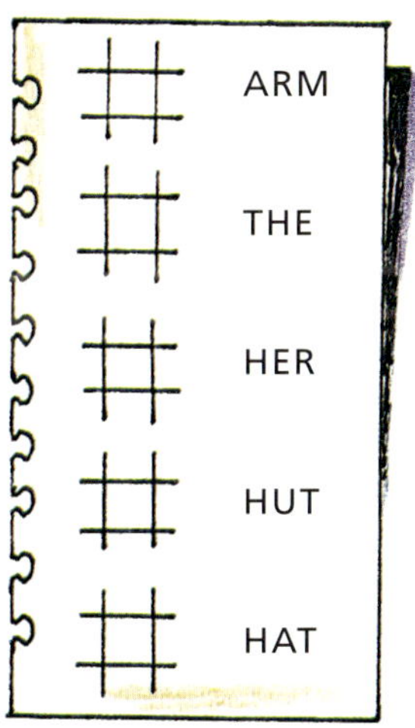

17 A pop magazine

Das Datum von heute

Interview with a pop star; a love song

Mr Plotter macht für die Popzeitschrift „Teens" ein Interview mit dem bekannten Sänger Giggi Fuzzy. Kreise die richtigen Wörter ein. So findest du die richtigen Lösungsbuchstaben für das Rätsel rechts.

Reporter: Hello, Giggi. Nice to meet you. A lot of **1)** – *young* **(L)** – ill **(H)** – *clever* **(B)** people like your **2)** – *car* **(R)** – *music* **(O)** – *house* **(C)**. Your **3)** – *mother* **(S)** – *father* **(M)** – *fans* **(T)** are interested in your **4)** – *private life* **(O)** – *books* **(K)** – *bike* **(S)**. Do you have a **5)** – *TV at home* **(V)** – *girlfriend* **(F)** – *stereo* **(G)**?

Giggi: A lot of girls want to be my girlfriend. They write **6)** – *love letters* **(N)** – *detective stories* **(B)** – *essays* **(F)** to me in which they ask the same question.

Reporter: So what? Who is your girlfriend?

Giggi: Well, I really like **7)** – *people* **(C)** – *strangers* **(D)** – *girls* **(I)**. I like girls with blonde hair. But girls with dark hair are great, too.

Reporter: Is your girlfriend blonde or dark haired?

Giggi: It isn't **8)** – *important* **(C)** – *boring* **(L)** – *nice* **(G)** what colour her hair is. It's the **9)** – *height* **(O)** – *character* **(E)** – *nose* **(M)** that counts.

Reporter: Has your girlfriend got a good character?

Giggi: A lot of girls have got a good character. Otherwise they wouldn't be my **10)** – *enimies* **(N)** – *relatives* **(V)** – *friends* **(S)** .

Reporter: Where did you meet her?

Giggi: I meet a lot of girls every day, and I love to go out with a **11)** – *stupid* **(O)** – *simple* **(T)** – *good looking* **(I)** girl at night.

Reporter: Where are you going to spend your next **12)** – *holiday* **(N)** – *workshop* **(E)** – *night* **(R)** together?

Giggi: Two weeks in Australia: sunshine, surfing and having **13)** – *fun* **(G)** – *money* **(J)** – *a cat* **(D)**, that would be great.
Well, I have to catch my **14)** – *dog* **(W)** – *plane* **(L)** – *ferry* **(E)** to Los Angeles now. The next concert is at three o'clock.

Reporter: Thank you very much for the **15)** – *coffee* **(U)** – *music* **(W)** – *interview* **(E)**.

What did the reporter find out? Has Giggi got a girlfriend:

Giggi knows a ___ ___ ___   ___ ___   ___ ___ ___ ___ girls.
1 2 3   4 5   6 7 8 9

But at the moment he is ___ ___ ___ ___ ___ ___.
10 11 12 13 14 15

The To-to love song

Streiche die überflüssigen „to". Wie viele „to" findest du?

You are like a tear in my eye.
I witoll nevetor tocryto
betocautose then I woultod lotose ytoou.

You are like the air in my lungs.
I will never bretoathe outto
tobecautose thtoen I wtoould loseto toyou.

You are like the hair on my head.
I wtoill netover cutto itto
betocatouse then I woutold lostoe yotou.

You are like a dream at night.
ToI witoll ntoever watoke up
bectoause theton I wtoould ltoose you.

You are like the sun in the sky.
I hotope itto will ntoever gtoo dotown
becautose thento Ito wotoould lotose you.

Es gibt _______ „to" in dem Song.

18 In a clothes shop

Das Datum von heute ____________

A sorting game; sizes; a shopping dialogue

Beschrifte die T-Shirts in der richtigen Farbe.

red						

Beschrifte die Sachen auf dem Wühltisch und sortiere sie danach alphabetisch (Nr. ① = A).

Franzy braucht eine neue Schuluniform.
Trage ein, was sie zu der Verkäuferin sagt.

I think size 12 is okay. – Hello, I'm looking for a new school uniform. – Yes, it's fine. Now, where do I find skirts? – I need a grey skirt, a blue blazer, a black pullover and a white blouse. – Okay, I'll take the blazer, the grey skirt and two white blouses. – Okay, I'll take it, too. Thank you for your help. – How much is this black pullover? – Can I try it on? – How does this skirt look on me?

Shop assistant: Hello, what can I do for you?

Franzy: ______________________________

Shop assistant: Okay, what do you need?

Franzy: ______________________________

Shop assistant: So let's start with the blazer. What size do you need?

Franzy: ______________________________

Shop assistant: Try this one.

Franzy: ______________________________

Shop assistant: Our skirts are over here.

Franzy: (She tries on a grey skirt.) ______________________________

Shop assistant: It looks great on you and these white blouses are really nice, too.

Franzy: ______________________________

Shop assistant: What else do you need? I can show you some nice pullovers.

Franzy: ______________________________

Shop assistant: It's £26.

Franzy: ______________________________

Shop assistant: Yes, of course.

Franzy: ______________________________

Shop assistant: You are welcome.

Das Datum von heute ____________

19 Road safety

Check your bike, bike safety rules

Verbinde die englischen Wörter mit den richtigen deutschen Übersetzungen. Die Buchstaben, die du dabei durchkreuzt, trage unten in den wichtigen Lösungssatz ein.

frame	1	A		Gabel
saddle	2	W I		Lenker
handlebar	3	L		Vorderlicht
front brake	4	W A		Reifen
back brake	5			Speiche
flag	6	A		Rahmen
front light	7	Y		Pedale
rear light	8			Rückbremse
tyre	9	E B S		Schutzblech
rain jacket	10			Sattel
pedals	11	K		Fahne
fork	12			Gangschaltung
spoke	13	E R		Vorderbremse
mudguard	14	T		Rücklicht
reflectors	15			Klingel
basket	16	H L		Schloss
bell	17	E		Regenjacke
chain	18	M		Kette
lock	19	E		Korb
gear shift	20			Reflektoren

Was musst du beim Radfahren immer tragen?

You must __ __ __ __ __ __   __ __ __ __
1 2 3 4 5 6   7 8 9 10

A __ __ __ __   __ __ __ __ __ __.
11 12 13 14   15 16 17 18 19 20

Beschrifte hier alle Dinge, die zu einem verkehrssicheren Fahrrad gehören. Welche sechs Dinge sind zwar sehr nützlich, gehören aber nicht unbedingt an ein verkehrssicheres Fahrrad?
Die Tabelle auf der vorherigen Seite hilft dir.

Jemand hat hier zu viel Luft in die Fahrradfahr-Regeln gepumpt. Entferne alle überflüssigen *ffff* und schreibe die wichtigen Regeln auf ein extra Blatt.

Bike Safety:

a) Alwfayffs kffeefp yfour efffyes fopen.
b) Tufrn youfffr ligffhts onf aft nifgfht.
c) Usef aff bfike paffth.
d) Doffn't rfifde thfe wrfofng waffy ifn a stffreet.
e) Doffn't rifde onf thffe pavffemefnt.
f) fWffear brffight cloftfhes sfo thffat drfifvers cfan sfefe yofu.

20 An accident

Das Datum von heute ______

A mind map; prepositions; in hospital

Vervollständige die Wörter, dann setze sie in das Wortnetz ein.

POLICE – ladder – police officer – fire – police station – FIRE BRIGADE – wheelchair – doctor – dangerous driver – hurt – hospital – AMBULANCE – injuries – paramedic – broken leg – accident – red – DIAL 999

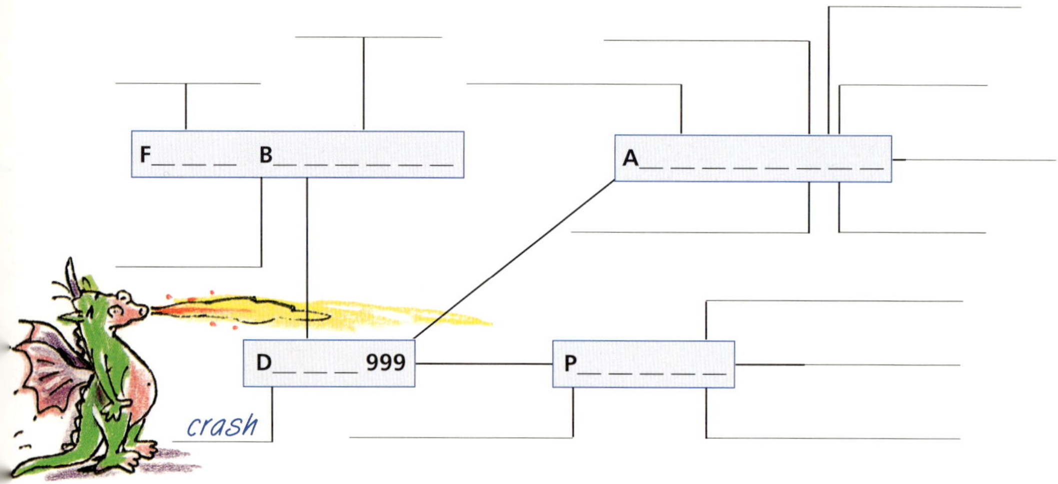

Vervollständige die Sätze mit den richtigen Präpositionen.

a) He died ______ a fever in hospital yesterday. **b)** I get fed ______ with stupid car drivers. **c)** I feel sorry ______ Peter. He is in hospital again. **d)** The motorbike crashed ____________ the car in front. **e)** My father had an accident when he went ________________ the road to the other side. **f)** The police asked the boy on the bike _______________ the accident.

Im Krankenhaus. Was ist passiert? Wer ist wer?
Ordne den Sätzen unten die richtige Nummer zu und vervollständige sie.

☐ I fell off a ladder and now I ______________________________.

☐ I had a bike accident and now I ______________________________.

☐ I played golf and now ______________________________.

☐ An elephant stood on my toe and now I ______________________________.

☐ I hit my finger with a hammer and now ______________________________.

☐ I had a car accident and now I ______________________________.

☐ I fell and now ______________________________.

☐ I played football and now ______________________________.

21 Body parts

Das Datum von heute

Naming; Guessing

Benenne die Körperteile.

arm, mouth, nose, hair, feet, arm, leg, hip, neck, toes, shoulder, eye, ear, knees

Vervollständige die Beschreibungen.

a) It has four ________ and two very big ________ on the left and the right of its ________ to hear with. It has very small ________ to see with.

b) It has a very long ____________ and four very long ____________.

c) It has two short __________ with big ___________ to help it swim.

d) It has a long tail* and two long ___________ and it can climb fast.

e) It has two long ____________ and a small tail.

f) It has four strong _____________ and it can run fast. It has strong ____________ in its ______________ to eat with.

g) It has four very short _______, two very small _______to see with and a very fat _____________ with a tail at the end.

h) It has four strong ________________ to run fast and lots of sharp ______________ in its _______________to eat its food.

i) It has a long _________, and no ___________.

j) It has four ________ and a long _________ with a head at the end. It has two small ___________ to see with.

* *tail* = Schwanz

22 Describing a person

Das Datum von heute

Funny person; who is who?

Wähle für die Personenbeschreibung die richtigen Adjektive aus und trage die Lösungsbuchstaben ins Lösungswort ein.

This funny fellow has got a **1.** **(W)** square – **(G)** round head.
His eyes are **2.** **(O)** big – **(A)** small. He has got a **3.** **(N)** long – **(B)** short nose.
Look at his ears. They are really **4.** **(B)** normal – **(D)** funny. He has got **5.** **(S)** nice – **(E)** awful hair. There is one thing I like about him: He looks **6.** **(R)** friendly – **(U)** angry. But his feet! Wow, they are so **7.** **(K)** clean – **(F)** dirty.
His hands are too **8.** **(H)** small – **(U)** large. Look at his legs: How **9.** **(L)** thin – **(D)** thick they are.

Welcome to the 'Funny People's Club,'

Mr ___ ___ ___ ___ ___ ___ ___ ___ ___!
1 2 3 4 5 6 7 8 9

Du bist Detektiv bzw. Detektivin!
Ordne den vier Fotos die jeweils passenden Personenbeschreibungen zu. Schreibe die Namen der Personen unter die Fotos.

①

②

③

④

Mr Brown is quite tall.
He has got dark hair.
He wears bright clothes.
His nose is very big.
His right arm is a bit longer than his left arm.

Mr Barker's ears are big.
He isn't very tall.
His face is oval.
He is quite fat.
He wears fashionable cool clothes.

Mr Benson has got a round face. He has got dark long hair.
He wears dark clothes.
His legs are very short but his arms are long.

Mr Botter has got dark hair.
His nose is quite long. And his ears are large.
His eyes are big.
He wears old clothes.

23 Arts and crafts

Das Datum von heute ____________

Bits of phrases; translation; removing extra letters

Jemand hatte Spaß am Schnippeln. Jetzt fehlt den Wortgruppen ihr Anfang. Klebe sie bitte wieder richtig zusammen.

on | **for** | **in** | **at**

______ the moment; ______ once; ______ home; ______ night;
______ six o'clock; ______ English; ______ 1654; ______ the country;
______ the morning; ______ the photo; ______ the street;
______ the beach; ______ 12th July; ______ the bus;
______ the table; ______ TV; ______ Monday; ______ tea;
______ example; ______ a long time; ______ weeks

Bastele eine Papiergirlande, indem du die Wörter übersetzt und sie in ein passendes Girlandenteil schreibst.

Entferne alle überflüssigen „ffs“ und du erhältst einen Satz:

FFFIFFFFYFFFOFFFFFUFFFFFWFFFFFAFFFFFNFTFFFTOFFFFFFMAFFFFKFFFFEFA
FFFFCFFARFFFFDFFFFFORFFFFSFOFFMEFFFBFFOFFFDYFFFYOFFFFUFFFNFFEFF
EDFFFCFFAFFRFFFDFFFFBOFFFFAFFFRFFFFD, FFEFLFFTFFFTFFFIFFPS,
FSCIFFFFSFSFORFFFS, FFGLFFFFUEFFFFAFFNFFDAFFGFOOFFFFDIFFF
DFFFEFFFA!!!!

Lösungssatz:

If ____

____

____.

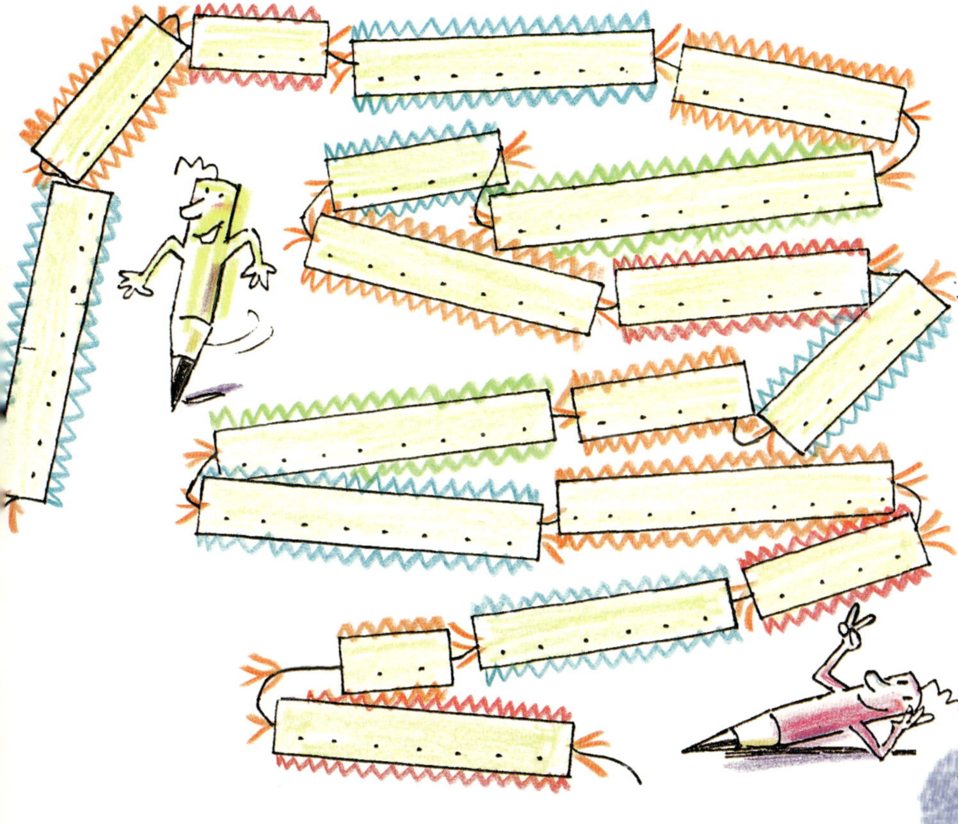

24 Irregular verbs

Das Datum von heute

Word game

Setze die Wörter aus der Verbenschlange an die richtige Stelle in der Tabelle.

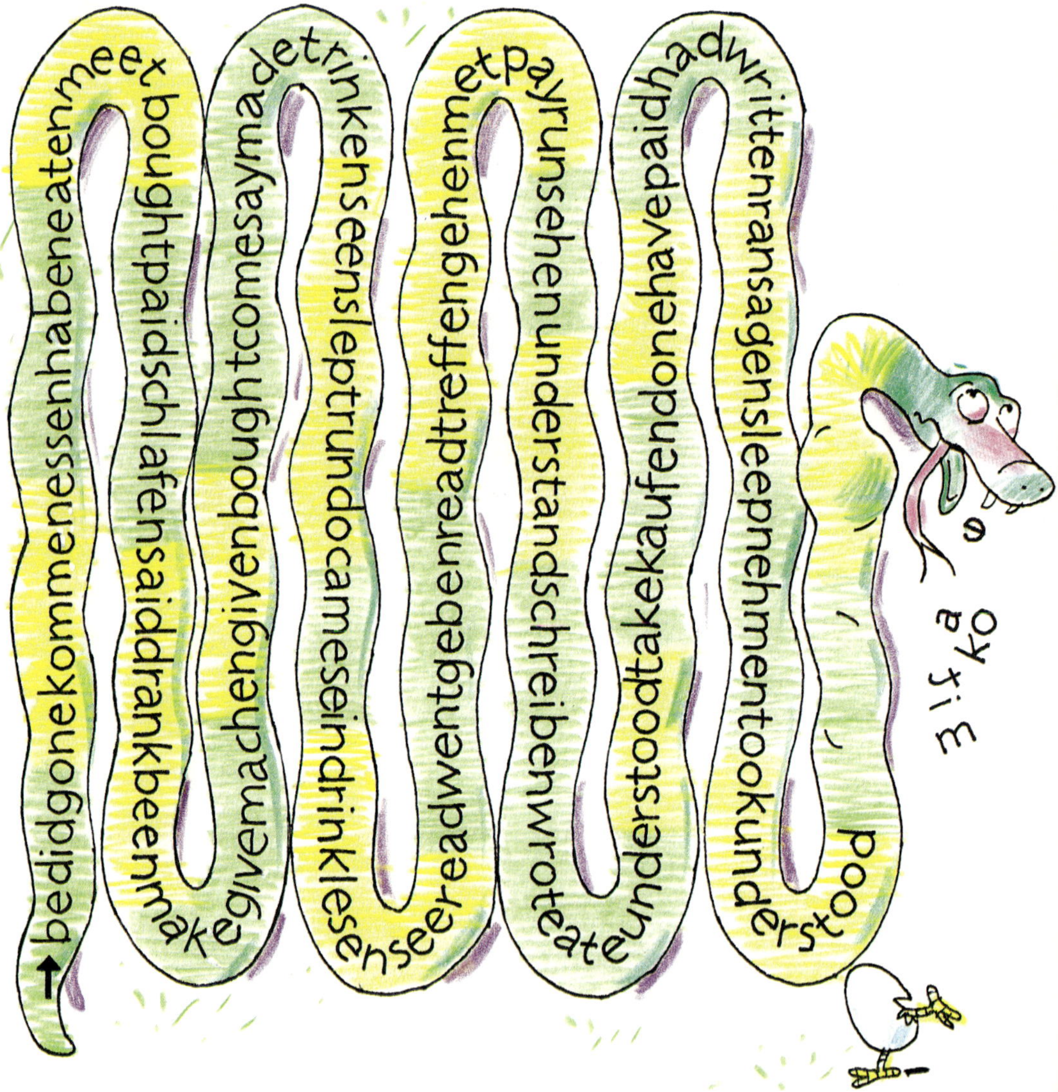

Infinitive	Simple past	Past participle	German
	was / were		
buy			
		come	
			tun
		drunk	
eat			
	gave		
go			
	had		
		made	
	met		
			bezahlen
read			
			rennen
		said	
	saw		
	slept		
		taken	
			verstehen
write			

25 A day trip

Das Datum von heute

____

A picture story

Ersetze im Text die Bilder durch die richtigen Wörter.
Bringe dann die Geschichte in die passende Reihenfolge.
Sallys Fotos auf der nächsten Seite helfen dir dabei.

river – village – bike – picnic – park – barbecue – island – rowing boats – lake

◯ They rode along a ______________  on a nice bike path. ◯ The children left their bikes near the café and rowed to the little island where they had a __________ . ◯ At lunchtime they stopped in a __________  where they had a ______________ . ◯ The owner told them: "You haven't locked your bike. So I kept it in my café for you. ◯ Last week Sally and her friends Janet, Tim and Alan went on a ___________  ride. ◯ In the park there was a ____________ . Near a café they saw a sign: _________________  for rent." In the middle of the lake there was a small ______________ . ◯ In the evening they got back to the café. ◯ They saw a nice ____________  with a little harbour. They had a look at the boats. ◯ Before the children went home, he invited them to a nice piece of strawberry cake. ◯ Alan noticed that his bike was gone. So they went into the café.

Ein paar Tage später klebt Sally ihre Fotos auf und schreibt Erinnerungen dazu. Hilf ihr dabei.

Last week me and my friends Janet, Tim and Alan went on a bike tour.

26 The environment

Das Datum von heute

Translating words; word search

Übersetze das erste Wort. In dem nächsten Wort findest du alle Buchstaben für die englische Übersetzung. Kreise diese ein. Die Buchstaben, die übrig bleiben, ergeben wieder das nächste Wort, das du übersetzen sollst.

U M W E L T

E V E R N V S C H I M R U O T N M Z E N E N T

W I E P D O L E R L V E U R T W E E R T U N G

R S E O N C N E Y N C E N E R L G I N I E G

S O W L A A R → E N L E R G D Y

S A F O U R E R E R S R E T G E N

A F C I A D → R B A R I I K N

M F Ü L A C L T T O O N R N E Y

R E B T T I E N N

K R S A V A F T E W E R K

A L P T O G L W A S E R → S C O T N T A T A I I N E R O N

B O T T L E B A N K

In diesem Suchrätsel sind zwölf englische Umweltwörter versteckt.
Suche sie heraus und ordne sie alphabetisch.

s	z	g	n	o	c	e	a	n	w	s
c	z	n	r	a	p	o	c	c	a	u
e	u	o	h	b	o	h	j	w	t	n
n	h	i	y	t	l	z	k	o	e	h
e	r	s	e	r	l	e	q	r	r	b
r	i	e	k	e	u	k	s	l	i	e
g	v	q	f	e	t	e	p	d	c	a
y	e	l	x	s	l	g	u	j	h	c
x	r	q	q	f	o	r	e	s	t	h
l	c	o	s	x	n	v	a	o	x	l
r	n	n	m	g	r	o	u	n	d	j

1. ______________________ 7. ______________________

2. ______________________ 8. ______________________

3. ______________________ 9. ______________________

4. ______________________ 10. ______________________

5. ______________________ 11. ______________________

6. ______________________ 12. ______________________

Setze aus jedem Wort unten einen Buchstaben ein und finde so den Lösungssatz (z. B.: 3/5 bedeutet = 3. Wort / 5. Buchstabe):

___ ___ ___ ___   ___ ___ ___   ___ ___ ___ ___ ___ !

3/5 1/3 8/3 10/3   6/1 9/2 11/5   12/1 5/2 2/4 7/3 4/6

27 Partners and opposites

Das Datum von heute

Working with words

Mache aus zwei Wörtern ein neues. Nimm dafür ein Wort aus dem ersten und ein Wort aus dem zweiten Koffer. Es werden 28 neue Wörter.

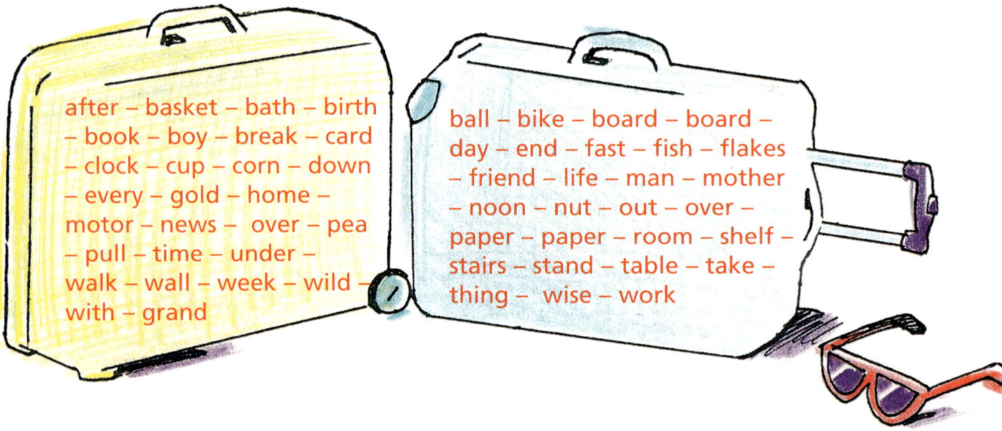

Finde das Gegenteil. Die Striche geben die Anzahl der Buchstaben an.
Schreibe das Lösungswort unten auf.

1. after → ___ ___ ___ ☐ ___ ___   **2.** far → ___ ☐ ___ ___

3. behind → ___ ___   ___ ☐ ___ ___ ___   ___ ___   **4.** up → ☐ ___ ___ ___

5. clean → ___ ___ ☐ ___ ___   **6.** expensive → ___ ___ ___ ☐ ___

7. safe → ___ ___ ___ ☐ ___ ___ ___ ___ ___

8. same → ___ ___ ___ ___ ___ ___ ☐ ___ ___

9. first → ☐ ___ ___ ___   **10.** difficult → ☐ ___ ___ ___

11. sad → ___ ___ ___ ___ ☐   **12.** thirsty → ___ ☐ ___ ___ ___ ___

13. short → ☐ ___ ___ ___   **14.** better → ☐ ___ ___ ___ ___

15. large → ___ ___ ☐ ___ ___   **16.** always → ☐ ___ ___ ___ ___

17. exciting → ___ ☐ ___ ___ ___ ___   **18.** dry → ___ ☐ ___

19. tidy → ___ ___ ☐ ___ ___ ___

Lösungssatz:

___ ___ ___ ___   ___ ___ ___ ___ !!!!!   ___ ___ ___
14 2 9 13   4 1 16 18   11 17 12

___ ___ ___   ___ ___ ___ ___ ___ !
15 3 10   7 5 8 6 19

28 Test

Das Datum von heute

____

Odd man out.
In jeder Reihe ist ein Wort, das nicht passt. Streiche es durch.

a) scarf, bikini, pullover, coat
b) swimming trunks, dress, skirt, bikini
c) shorts, trousers, shirt, jeans
d) swimming trunks, sandals, swimsuit, bikini
e) sweatshirt, pullover, jacket, trousers

Für jedes richtig gefundene Wort erhältst du einen Punkt.

Ich habe ___ Punkte.

Sort the things.
Die 15 Wörter müssen richtig einsortiert werden.

handlebar – toes – teeth – trousers – coat – frame – shoes – scarf – eyes – leg – brakes – tyre – jeans – hair – pedals

My clothes	My bike	My body

Für jedes richtig gefundene Wort erhältst du einen Punkt.

Ich habe ___ Punkte.

Mixed pictures. Welcher Text passt zu welchem Bild? Verbinde.

Ⓐ There are an ambulance and a police car. The bike is under the car. Two people must go to hospital.

Ⓑ There's an ambulance. Two men are helping the boy on the ground. The car crashed into the bike.

Ⓒ Two boys are hurt. One was on a bike and one on a motorbike. The police car is blocking the road.

Für jeden richtig zugeordneten Text erhältst du zwei Punkte.

Ich habe ___ Punkte.

Irregular verbs. Suche die Fehler, die sich hier eingeschlichen haben.

gehen	goh	went	gon
sagen	saiy	said	sait
schreiben	wite	wrote	writen
lesen	read	read	readen
kaufen	by	bought	bought

Für jeden gefundenen Fehler erhältst du einen Punkt. Ich habe ____ Punkte.

Addiere deine Punkte aus allen 4 Übungen. Ich habe _____ Punkte insgesamt.

Mehr als 29 Punkte: Deine Leistung ist sehr gut. Mehr als 25 Punkte: Deine Leistung ist gut. Mehr als 20 Punkte: In Ordnung! Mehr als 16 Punkte: Es könnte besser sein! Weniger als 15 Punkte: Du solltest die Kapitel 17 – 27 noch einmal wiederholen!

29 Take a break

Das Datum von heute

____

Making and playing a game

Jetzt kannst du mit zwei oder drei Freunden das Umweltspiel basteln und spielen. Du brauchst einen Würfel und Spielpüppchen. Schneide die Handlungskärtchen aus (oder schreibe die Texte auf kleine Kärtchen) und lege sie verdeckt (mit der Vorderseite nach unten) auf das Spielfeld. Immer wenn du auf ein Stoppschild triffst, musst du eine Karte ziehen und die Anweisungen befolgen.

You take your bottles to a bottle bank. Throw again.	You use your bike to go to town. Go on 3 spaces.	You use solar energy at home. Throw again.	You work in a "Green team". Go on 2 spaces.	You sort out your rubbish. Go on 2 spaces.
You throw your rubbish in the street. Miss a turn.	Your motor bike is losing oil. Go back 3 spaces.	A factory pollutes the river. Miss 2 turns.	There's a lot of acid rain. Go back 2 spaces.	There's too much traffic in the city. Go back 3 spaces.

Cornelsen

Jeden Tag ein bisschen besser

Damit klappt das Lernen spielend! Jedes Heft bietet zu wichtigen schulischen Themen kurze Trainingseinheiten für 15–30 Minuten täglich. So werden die „Denkmuskeln" fit gehalten und das Wissen wird vertieft. Jedes Heft ist vierfarbig und enthält einen heraustrennbaren Lösungsteil.

Darum ab sofort: **Jeden Tag ein bisschen besser …**

… im Fach	ISBN 3-589-
Deutsch	
4. Schuljahr	21190-3
5. Schuljahr	21191-1
6. Schuljahr	21193-8
7. Schuljahr	21194-6
Übungsdiktate	
4. Schuljahr	21375-2
5. Schuljahr	21243-8
6. Schuljahr	21244-6
7. Schuljahr	21376-0

Für alle Fächer

Lernen, so geht's!	
5./6. Schuljahr	21373-6
7./8. Schuljahr	21374-4

… im Fach	ISBN 3-589-
Mathematik	
4. Schuljahr	21202-0
5. Schuljahr	21203-9
6. Schuljahr	21204-7
7. Schuljahr	21205-5
8. Schuljahr	21206-3
Testaufgaben	
5. Schuljahr	21355-8
6. Schuljahr	21356-6
7. Schuljahr	22123-2
8. Schuljahr	22124-0
Englisch	
5. Schuljahr	21196-2
6. Schuljahr	21197-0
7. Schuljahr	21198-9
8. Schuljahr	21199-7
Vokabeltrainer	
4. Schuljahr	22069-4
5. Schuljahr	22070-8
6. Schuljahr	22071-6

Fragen Sie bitte in Ihrer Buchhandlung oder im gut sortierten Fachhandel!